Readers' Theater: How to Put on a Production

Turkey and Takeout

A Readers' Theater Script and Guide

Looking Glass Library

An Imprint of Magic Wagon
abdopublishing.com

By Nancy K. Wallace   Illustrated by Lucy Fleming

To my mother, Ann Kennedy, who made every holiday magical. —NKW

abdopublishing.com

Published by Magic Wagon, a division of ABDO, PO Box 398166, Minneapolis, Minnesota 55439.
Copyright © 2016 by Abdo Consulting Group, Inc. International copyrights reserved in all countries. No part of this book may be reproduced in any form without written permission from the publisher. Looking Glass Library™ is a trademark and logo of Magic Wagon.

Printed in the United States of America, North Mankato, Minnesota.
042015
092015

THIS BOOK CONTAINS RECYCLED MATERIALS

Written by Nancy K. Wallace
Illustrations by Lucy Fleming
Edited by Heidi M.D. Elston, Megan M. Gunderson & Bridget O'Brien
Designed by Laura Mitchell

Library of Congress Cataloging-in-Publication Data

Wallace, Nancy K.
  Turkey and takeout : a readers' theater script and guide / by Nancy K. Wallace ; illustrated by Lucy Fleming.
    pages cm. -- (Readers' theater : how to put on a production set 2)
  ISBN 978-1-62402-117-6
1. Thanksgiving Day--Juvenile drama. 2. Children's plays, American. 3. Theater--Production and direction--Juvenile literature. 4. Readers' theater--Juvenile literature. I. Fleming, Lucy, illustrator. II. Title.
  PS3623.A4436T87 2016
  812'.6--dc23
                    2015002813

Table of Contents

Celebrate with a Play!

Everyone loves holidays! Some schools and libraries hold programs or assemblies to commemorate special occasions. This series offers fun plays to help celebrate six different holidays at your school or library. You can even sell tickets and use your play as a fund-raiser.

Readers' theater can be done very simply. The performers sit on stools or chairs onstage. They don't have to memorize their lines. They just read them.

Adapted readers' theater looks more like a regular play. The stage includes scenery and props. The performers wear makeup and costumes. They move around to show the action. But, they still carry their scripts.

Readers' theater scripts can also be used for puppet shows. The performers stand behind a curtain, move the puppets, and read their scripts.

Find a place large enough to put on a play. An auditorium with a stage is ideal. A classroom will work, too. Choose a date and ask permission to use the space. Advertise your play with posters and flyers. Place them around your school and community. Tell your friends and family. Everyone enjoys watching a fun performance!

Tickets and Playbills

Tickets and playbills can be handwritten or designed on a computer. Be sure tickets include the title of the play. They should list the date, time, and location of the performance.

A playbill is a printed program. The front of a playbill has the title of the play, the date, and the time. The cast and crew are listed inside. Be sure to have enough playbills for the audience and cast. Pass them out at the door as the audience enters.

The Crew

Next, a crew is needed. The show can't go on without these important people! Some jobs can be combined for a small show.

Director — organizes everyone and everything in the show.

Costume Designer — designs and borrows or makes all the costumes.

Stage Manager — makes sure everything runs smoothly.

Lighting Designer — runs spotlights and other lighting.

Set Designer — plans and makes scenery.

Prop Manager — finds, makes, and keeps track of props.

Special Effects Crew — takes care of sound and other special effects.

Sets

At a readers' theater production, the performers can sit on stools at the front of the room. An adapted readers' theater production or full play will require sets and props. A set is the background that creates the setting for each scene. A prop is an item the actors use onstage.

Scene 1 takes place outside. Make a backdrop of painted trees. This scene can also take place in front of the closed curtains on a stage, which allows stage crew to set up for scene 2.

Scene 2 is in Maddy's kitchen. It needs a backdrop showing a sink, a counter, and cupboards. There should also be a table and three chairs.

Scene 3 is in Grandpa's house. It needs a small sofa, a rug, and a low table.

Scene 4 takes place inside the homeless shelter. Use two tables for serving tables. Set two more tables diagonally at stage left and stage right.

Scene 5 is just outside the shelter, which can be painted on cardboard. Use a portable fire pit with paper flames so the characters can roast marshmallows.

Props

- Big basket
- Rake
- Artificial leaves
- Plates
- Silverware
- Magazine
- Coffee mug

- Plate of cookies
- Glass of milk
- Serving bowls
- Big pots
- Serving spoons
- Bowl of mashed potatoes
- Napkins

- Box of disposable pie pans
- Aluminum foil
- Sticks for roasting marshmallows
- Marshmallows

The Cast

Decide who will play each part. Each person in the cast will need a script. All of the performers should practice their lines. Reading lines aloud over and over will help the performers learn them. *Turkey and Takeout* needs the following cast:

Maddy Duncan — a girl who loves Thanksgiving

Grandpa — Maddy's grandfather

Tara — Maddy's friend

Mr. Marsh — man in charge of the shelter

Mrs. Duncan — Maddy's mom

Mr. Duncan — Maddy's dad

Person 1 — comes to Thanksgiving dinner

Person 2 — comes to Thanksgiving dinner

Person 3/Uncle Danny — Maddy's uncle

Makeup and Costumes

Makeup artists have a big job! Every cast member wears makeup. And, stage makeup needs to be brighter and heavier than regular makeup. Buy several basic shades of mascara, foundation, blush, and lipstick. Apply with a new cotton ball or swab for each cast member to avoid spreading germs.

Costume designers set the scene just as much as set designers. They borrow costumes or adapt old clothing for each character. Ask adults for help finding and sewing costumes.

Most of the performers in this play can wear regular clothes they would wear to school. There are a couple exceptions.

Uncle Danny needs a hooded sweatshirt decorated like a turkey.

Grandpa should apply "wrinkles" using an eyebrow pencil. He could even wear a bald cap and a fake beard!

Rehearsals and Stage Directions

After you decide to put on a play, it is important to set up a rehearsal schedule. Choose a time everyone can attend, such as after school or on weekends. Try to have at least five rehearsals before the performance.

Everyone should practice together as a team, even though individual actors will be reading their own scripts. This will help the play sound like a conversation, instead of separate lines. Onstage, actors should act like their characters even when they aren't speaking.

In the script, stage directions are in parentheses. They are given from the performer's point of view, not the audience's. Actors face the audience when performing, so left is on their left and right is on their right.

Some theater terms may be unfamiliar:

Curtains — the main curtain at the front of the stage.

House — the area in which the audience sits.

Wings — the part of the stage on either side that the audience can't see.

Stage
Left

Downstage

Stage
Right

Center Stage

Left Wing

Upstage

Right Wing

Script: Turkey and Takeout
Scene 1: Outside Tara's House

(Maddy and Tara need a basket and a rake. Scatter artificial colored leaves around the stage. The girls should pick up and rake the leaves and put them in the basket as they are talking. Use a tree backdrop or stand-up fake trees.)

Maddy: I love Thanksgiving! I'm so glad it's next week!

Tara: *(Throws little handfuls of leaves into the air.)* Turkey, mashed potatoes, and pumpkin pie! Yum!

Maddy: You should try my grandpa's mashed potatoes. I think he uses cream cheese!

Tara: My grandma makes awesome pumpkin pie and apple pie.

Maddy: We always have apple pie, too, and sometimes pecan pie. My dad loves that.

Tara: *(Makes a face.)* Ick! Too many nuts.

Maddy: After dinner, my uncle Danny makes up a treasure hunt for all the kids. We get clues that take us all over the house and even outside. Whoever finds the treasure first gets to keep it. Last year, I won!

Tara: That sounds like more fun than doing dishes. I always get stuck helping with those. Everyone else at my house hangs out in the living room, snoring and watching football.

Maddy: We all go for a walk when the dishes are done. It's usually a little cold. One year we even had snow flurries! When we come back, Daddy lights a fire in the fireplace and we make s'mores, pop popcorn, and tell stories.

Tara: Okay, the Duncans win the Family of the Year award! That sounds so nice. Can I come to your house for Thanksgiving?

Maddy: Sure! That would be fun!

Tara: Just kidding. I'd really like to, but my mom would be upset. My family likes to have everything just the same every year. It's tradition and all that. *(Rolls her eyes.)*

Maddy: I know what you mean. My family is that way, too. It's kind of nice, though. I look forward to it every year. If something changed, it just wouldn't be the same!

Mrs. Duncan: *(Calling from offstage.)* Maddy! Are you almost finished? Dinner's ready!

Maddy: I'd better go.

Tara: I can finish this.

Maddy: *(Throws a handful of leaves at Tara.)* See you tomorrow!

Scene 2: Maddy's Kitchen

(Set the stage with a table and three chairs. A painted backdrop should show a sink, a counter, and cupboards. Mrs. Duncan is putting plates on the table. Maddy enters from stage right.)

Mrs. Duncan: Hi, honey! Wash your hands, and then could you set the table for me?

Maddy: Sure! *(Maddy pretends to wash her hands at the sink.)*

Mrs. Duncan: Did you get the leaves in Tara's yard raked?

Maddy: Some of them. We were mostly throwing them around.

Mrs. Duncan: *(She hands Maddy some silverware.)* Well it sounds like you had fun!

Maddy: We were talking about Thanksgiving. *(She spins around and hugs herself.)* I *love* Thanksgiving!

Mrs. Duncan: *(Stops and hesitates.)* This year, Thanksgiving will be especially awesome!

Maddy: *(Stops twirling and sounds puzzled.)* Why? What's going to be different?

Mrs. Duncan: We're volunteering at the homeless shelter on Fifth Street.

Maddy: (*Staring at her mother.*) Who's volunteering?

Mrs. Duncan: You and Daddy and I! We're going to serve dinner all day to people who wouldn't have a Thanksgiving meal otherwise.

Maddy: (*Angrily.*) Why didn't you tell me? You didn't even ask me if I wanted to do that!

Mrs. Duncan: I'm sorry, honey. I didn't think I needed to. Daddy and I just decided last night. We were going to tell you tonight at dinner. I thought you would be excited to have a chance to help other people.

Maddy: (*Puts silverware down and folds her arms over her chest.*) I *do* want to help other people . . . just not on Thanksgiving.

Mrs. Duncan: (*Sounding offended.*) Maddy! Some people in our town don't have enough to eat. Do you want Thanksgiving to be just another day for them? Daddy and I thought this would be such a good way to give something back to the community.

Maddy: (*In a very soft voice.*) But I *love* Thanksgiving, Mom. I don't want it to be different this year. I want to have Thanksgiving dinner with just our family. I want Grandpa's mashed potatoes and your pumpkin pie. I want s'mores and stories and Uncle Danny's treasure hunt.

Mrs. Duncan: Maddy, it isn't as though Thanksgiving celebrations have always remained the same. At the first Thanksgiving celebration in Plymouth, they didn't have mashed potatoes or cranberry sauce or pumpkin pie. There may not even have been turkey.

Maddy: No turkey?

Mrs. Duncan: No, they had venison, which is deer meat. They were giving thanks for their first good harvest after not having enough to eat the year before. They invited the Wampanoag with their chief, Massasoit, to celebrate with them because they appreciated their help. Maddy, our Thanksgiving, which you love so much, isn't really traditional. Most people don't make s'mores or have a goofy uncle who plans Thanksgiving treasure hunts!

Maddy: I know Tara doesn't. She wanted to come to our house because our Thanksgiving sounded like so much fun.

Mrs. Duncan: Helping at the homeless shelter will be fun, too.

Maddy: But, it won't be the same!

Mrs. Duncan: No, it won't be the same. But it can still be a very nice holiday. Think how good you'll feel to be helping people. And you'll still be with your dad and me.

Maddy: *(Angrily.)* What if I hate it? What if Thanksgiving is *awful? (She exits stage right.)*

Mrs. Duncan: Maddy, come back! Daddy will be home in five minutes and dinner is ready.

Maddy: *(Yelling from offstage.)* I'm not hungry!

Scene 3: Grandpa's House

(Use a rug, a small sofa, and a side table or coffee table to set the scene. Put a plate of cookies on the coffee table. Grandpa sits in a chair reading a magazine and drinking coffee.)

(Maddy knocks from offstage. Grandpa gets up to open the door.)

Maddy: Hi, Grandpa.

Grandpa: *(Gives her a hug.)* Hi, Maddy!

Maddy: I asked Mom if I could stop by on my way home from school. She knows I'm here.

Grandpa: I know, she called me. She just wanted to make sure I would be home when you stopped by. I'm going to volunteer at the library at four o'clock, but that leaves a whole hour just for you! Come and sit down.

(Maddy follows him in but doesn't say anything else.)

Grandpa: *(Points at the coffee table.)* How about a glass of milk to go with these cookies?

Maddy: Okay. I do love pumpkin cookies.

(Grandpa exits stage left. He returns with a glass of milk and sets it on the coffee table.)

Grandpa: Is there something you'd like to talk about, Maddy?

Maddy: *(Nods her head.)* I want to talk about Thanksgiving. Mom said we're helping at the homeless shelter this year.

Grandpa: That's a really nice thing to do.

Maddy: I know it is, but I feel like it's going to ruin *our* Thanksgiving.

Grandpa: It's going to make a lot of people very happy.

Maddy: Not me. I'll miss your mashed potatoes and Mom's pie and just being together with everyone. It won't be the same.

Grandpa: I'll tell you something funny, Maddy. It's the holidays that are different that people remember best. All the ones that are the same kind of blend together.

Maddy: What do you mean?

Grandpa: Do you remember the year Uncle Danny dropped his marshmallow and set the rug on fire?

Maddy: *(Laughing.)* Yes! Daddy had to use the fire extinguisher!

Grandpa: And how about the year the treasure was a dozen giant gingerbread cookies and the dog gobbled them up before you found them?

Maddy: I remember that, too! All that was left was a slobbery bag. There weren't even any crumbs!

Grandpa: And how about two years ago when it snowed and the roads were so bad no one could drive home?

Maddy: All the kids slept on the living room floor and Uncle Danny told us ghost stories all night.

Grandpa: So every Thanksgiving hasn't been the same, has it?

Maddy: I guess not. But they were all fun!

Grandpa: That's right! They *were* all fun. And this one will be fun, too. Promise.

Scene 4: The Homeless Shelter

(Set the stage with two long tables with big pots, bowls, pie pans, and paper plates. Have two other tables set diagonally with tablecloths and silverware, one stage right and one stage left.)

(Maddy enters from stage right with her parents. Mrs. Duncan carries a box of pies.)

Mr. Marsh: Happy Thanksgiving! Thank you so much for coming along to help, Maddy.

Maddy: Happy Thanksgiving, Mr. Marsh.

Grandpa: *(Enters from stage left with a huge bowl of mashed potatoes.)* Happy Thanksgiving, all!

Maddy: Grandpa! What are you doing here? Why didn't you tell me you were coming?

Grandpa: I made the mashed potatoes. And I wanted to surprise you!

Maddy: *(Gives him a hug.)* I'm really glad you're here!

(Several people walk in from stage right.)

Mr. Marsh: It looks like people are ready to eat. Mr. Duncan, can you cut the pies and cakes and put them on paper plates? Then I'd love some help carving these turkeys.

Mr. Duncan: Sure! (*Goes over to the serving table.*)

Mr. Marsh: Mrs. Duncan, would you serve the corn and green beans?

Mrs. Duncan: I'd be glad to!

Grandpa: Maddy, you can serve the potatoes. And don't be stingy. There are plenty more in the kitchen.

Maddy: Okay!

Mr. Marsh: Let's get busy! And be sure to make everyone feel welcome.

(*The first people approach Maddy carrying plates, and Maddy pretends to serve them.*)

Maddy: Happy Thanksgiving! Would you like some mashed potatoes?

Person 1: Yes, please.

Maddy: Hello! Do you like mashed potatoes? My grandpa made them. They're so good!

Person 2: Thank you very much!

(*Person 3 approaches with a turkey costume on. The hood hides most of his face.*)

Maddy: (*Starts to laugh.*) Happy Thanksgiving, Mr. Turkey! Do you like mashed potatoes?

Person 3: Do you do takeout?

Maddy: Takeout? I don't know. Mr. Marsh, can we do takeout for this turkey?

Mr. Marsh: *(Laughing.)* Why not? How many meals do you need?

Person 3: *(Pulls down his hood.)* I'm just kidding, Maddy. It's me!

Maddy: Uncle Danny! I can't believe you came!

Uncle Danny: Well, this is where my family is. I think I should help, too. What can I do?

Mr. Marsh: Can you take over serving the stuffing? I'll go and greet people!

Uncle Danny: Sure thing! Then I'll be right beside my favorite niece! *(Leans over to Maddy and speaks in a stage whisper.)* Guess what! I thought maybe we could get all the kids to participate in a treasure hunt after dinner. I brought a nice treasure with me.

Maddy: Really?

Uncle Danny: Of course! It's tradition. And that's the kind of thing favorite uncles do. And I'm your favorite uncle, right?

Maddy: *(Smiling.)* Yes, you are!

Scene 5: Behind the Homeless Shelter

(Build the outside of the shelter out of cardboard or paint a backdrop. Set the stage with a portable fire pit. Put a string of orange or red lights in it to create a fire-like glow. Make flames out of paper. Have the cast stand around the fire pit in a semicircle, leaving the side toward the audience open.)

Uncle Danny: The fire is ready!

Maddy: Okay, everyone! *(Passing out sticks and marshmallows to the people gathered around.)* Be sure everyone gets a stick and some marshmallows!

(Danny and Maddy move toward stage right as the others roast marshmallows.)

Uncle Danny: So what do you think, Maddy? Was this the Thanksgiving you were dreading?

Maddy: *(Shaking her head.)* No way. I made some new friends. I got to be with my family. We had a great treasure hunt . . .

Uncle Danny: *(Pointing at Maddy.)* Which you could have won but didn't. I saw you hesitate and let that little boy go ahead of you.

Maddy: *(Embarrassed.)* Jake hadn't ever done a treasure hunt before. Did you see how excited he was when he won?

Uncle Danny: I did, and I'm very proud of you. I know you didn't want to do this today.

Maddy: You're right, I didn't. At least, not at first. But this Thanksgiving was very special. It made me feel good.

Uncle Danny: It made me feel good, too!

Maddy: After talking to everyone here, I'm really thankful I have a house and a bed and a family who loves me and . . . *(She stops and smiles.)* Grandpa's mashed potatoes!

Uncle Danny: They really are the best, aren't they? I think there are still some left in the kitchen. Do you want to go see if we can sneak a bowl of mashed potatoes for takeout?

Maddy: Sure! Happy Thanksgiving, Uncle Danny!

Uncle Danny: Happy Thanksgiving, Maddy!

The End

Adapting Readers' Theater Scripts

Readers' theater can be done very simply. Performers just read their lines from scripts. They don't have to memorize them! And, they don't have to move around. The performers sit on chairs or stools while reading their parts.

Adapted Readers' Theater: This looks more like a regular play. The performers wear makeup and costumes. The stage has scenery and props. The cast moves around to show the action. Performers can still read from their scripts.

A Puppet Show: Some schools and libraries have puppet collections. Or students can create puppets. Students make the puppets be the actors. They read their scripts for their puppets.

Teaching Guides

Readers' Theater Teaching Guides are available online at **abdopublishing.com**. Each guide includes printable scripts, reading levels for each character, and additional production tips for each play. Get yours today!

Websites

To learn more about Readers' Theater, visit **booklinks.abdopublishing.com**. These links are routinely monitored and updated to provide the most current information available.